BiG Thoughts for Little Thinkers

D0815570

ts inkers

BiG Thoughts for Little Thinkers

BiG Tho for Littl

BiG Thoughts for Little Thinkers

BiG Thoughts for Little Thinkers

ghts hinkers

BiG Thoughts for Little Thinkers

BiG Tho for Litt

BiG Thoughts for ittle Thinkers

BiG Thoughts for ittle Thinkers

BiG Thoughts for Little Thinkers

BiG Thoughts for Little Thinkers

ughts Thinkers

BiG Thoughts for Little Thinkers

BiG T Li

BiG Thoughts for Little Thinkers

BiG Thoughts for Little Thinkers

ughts e Thinkers

BiG Thoughts for Little Thinkers

BiG

BiG Thoughts for ittle Thinkers

BiG Thoughts for Little Thinkers

BiG Thoughts for Little Thinkers

THE SCRIPTURE
BY JOEY ALLEN

New Leaf Press
A Division of New Leaf Publishing Group

First Printing: March 2005
Seventh Printing: August 2018

New Leaf Press Inc., PO Box 726, Green Forest, AR 72638

New Leaf Press is a division of the New Leaf Publishing Group, Inc.

Illustrations and text by Joey Allen

Please consider requesting that a copy of this volume be purchased by your local library system.

For my dad

ISBN-13: 978-0-89221-615-4
ISBN-13: 978-1-61458-147-5 (digital)
Library of Congress Control Number: 2004118191
Printed in China

Please visit our website for other great titles:
www.newleafpress.net

For information regarding author interviews,
please contact the publicity department at (870) 438-5288.

FOREWORD

God intends for parents to be the primary educators of their children. A quick look at Deuteronomy 6 should be sufficient to indicate the seriousness with which God invests parents with this task. In everything we do, we are to teach and instruct our children in the wisdom of God.

Joey Allen has provided a helpful way for parents to teach the truths of God's Word to children. A gifted artist, he brings his considerable talent to this project and also demonstrates a wonderful heart for young children.

I am glad to see the profound truth of God's Word and the wonderful transforming truth of the Gospel of Jesus Christ presented to children in a way they can understand. The release of these books is good news for parents and good news for children.

By God's grace, let us determine to be faithful in teaching our children and to be careful to teach them the precious truths of God's Word. In so doing, let's start them on a path that will turn little theologians into faithful disciples.

– R. Albert Mohler, Jr.
President, The Southern Baptist Theological Seminary
Louisville, Kentucky

A WORD TO PARENTS AND TEACHERS

The Bible is an unparalleled document. No book in history has made a more profound impact on the world than the Bible. No book has ever been published more frequently or printed more often. Translations of the Bible exist in more than 2,000 languages, with new translations being produced every year. Scholars recognize the Bible as both a literary masterpiece and a priceless historical account, but these merits, while noteworthy, are dwarfed by the Bible's incomparably great worth as the very Word of God.

Children today are growing up in a world of chaos, a world filled with broken homes and unstable relationships. We must direct them to the firm foundation of God's timeless truth. This book attempts to introduce children to fundamental concepts about the Bible such as its heavenly source, trustworthiness and sufficiency, the centrality of

Christ, and the necessity of the Holy Spirit's assistance for proper interpretation. Use this book as a tool to help the next generation find wisdom that leads to salvation, guidance for everyday living, and hope for the future through the Bible.

My prayer is that this book will help children know and trust God through His Word.

—Joey Allen

Hi! My name is Gabe. I want to tell you about the Bible. The Bible is the most important book in the whole world! Do you know why the Bible is so important?

Pretend that no one ever talked to you. What if your parents never said anything to you or read books to you? What if no one taught you how to tie your shoes or say your ABCs? That would be very bad.

Even worse, what if God never spoke to you? What if God never told you about himself? What if the God who made you never told you how to live? That would be *terrible!*

Deuteronomy 4:5-14;
Psalm 28:1

But God has spoken! God wants you to know Him. But we can only know God if He tells us about himself.

Isaiah 1:2; 55:8; Daniel 2:22

God tells us about himself by the things that He made. I like looking through my telescope. I know that God is powerful and amazing when I look at the sky and see all the stars He has made.

Psalm 19:1; Romans 1:20

We learn some things about God by looking at the world, but we cannot learn everything God wants us to know. God wanted to tell us special things about himself, so He gave us the Bible. The Bible is important because God talks to us through the Bible!

1 Corinthians 2:6–13; Ephesians 1:9; 3:5; Isaiah 30:8

A long time ago, God began speaking to people. God chose some people to write down His words, and the Holy Spirit directed them as they wrote.

Exodus 24:4; Jeremiah 30:2; 2 Peter 1:20-21

At first, God chose to speak mainly to one group of people called "the people of Israel." The first part of the Bible is mostly their story. We call this part of the Bible the Old Testament.

Genesis 12:1–3; Exodus 19:1-9; 1 Corinthians 10:11

The Old Testament is full of stories that teach us about God. We learn that God is perfect and that He created a good world. But bad things happen in the world because people disobeyed God. But we also learn that God is loving, and He has a plan to make everything right again.

Genesis 1:31; 3:1-24; Isaiah 6:3; Jeremiah 31:31-34

In the Old Testament, God told people what would happen in the future. God promised that one day He would send a Savior. At just the right time, God the Father sent His Son to be born on earth. They named Him Jesus. The entire Old Testament points to Jesus.

Isaiah 7:14; 9:6-7; Luke 24:27; John 5:39; Galatians 4:4

When Jesus came to earth, He showed us what God is like. Jesus acted like God and talked like God because He is God! When we learn about Jesus in the Bible, we are learning about God.

John 1:18; 10:25, 30; 14:9; Colossians 2:9; Hebrews 1:2-3

The Holy Spirit chose some people to write books about Jesus' life on earth. The Holy Spirit led other people to write books explaining why Jesus came to earth and how to follow Him. These books are called the New Testament.

1 Corinthians 2:10-13;
1 Thessalonians 1:5-6

People who believed in Jesus gathered together all the books that came from God. They took the books from the Old Testament and the New Testament and put them into one book called the Bible.

God used about 40 people to write the Bible. For example, He used a doctor, a farmer, and even a fisherman. The Holy Spirit made sure that these people wrote exactly what He wanted them to write.

2 Timothy 3:16

The Bible is God's letter to us. It was first written in three languages, Hebrew, Greek, and Aramaic — but mostly in Hebrew and Greek. The Bible has been copied many times and into many languages, but God has always protected its message.

Matthew 5:18-19, Luke 16:17; John 10:35

No other book is like the Bible. As you read the Bible, you can tell that it came from God because it does not sound like something a human would make up.

John 10:27; 1 Corinthians 2:14; 1 Thessalonians 2:13

The Bible is so important because we cannot clearly know God without it. If we did not have the Bible, we would be in deep trouble because we would not know what to believe.

Psalm 119:165; Romans 10:14

Has anyone ever told you a lie? What if people told you it was cold outside, but really it was burning hot? It would be hard to trust someone who lied to you.

But God always speaks the truth, and He always keeps His promises. You can trust the Bible since God never lies. The Bible is full of God's promises that help you know what to do and where to go.

Numbers 23:19; Psalm 119:105; Titus 1:2; Hebrews 6:18

Every morning when you wake up, you can be happy because the Bible says God is with you, and one day you will be with Him in heaven.

John 14:1-3;
Hebrews 13:5-6

In the Bible, God tells you all the things He wants you to know. The Bible teaches you how to love God and other people. It helps you live a life that makes God happy!

Micah 6:8; Romans 14:18; Colossians 1:10; Hebrews 11:6

As you think about what you read in the Bible, it will change you. You will be happy if you believe God's Word and obey it.

Joshua 1:8; Psalm 19:7-11; Romans 12:1-2; 2 Corinthians 3:18

God loves you and wants you to grow as His child. The Bible will help you grow and protect you from sin and things that could hurt you.

Psalm 107:10–11; 119:9–11; 1 Timothy 4:15

Some things in the Bible are hard to understand. Do not worry. Jesus promised that He would send the Holy Spirit, and He will help you!

John 14:26; 16:7-15;
2 Peter 3:16

The Holy Spirit gives some people the ability to teach the Bible. Find someone who has been a Christian for a long time and ask him or her to help you understand the Bible.

Ephesians 4:10-12;
2 Timothy 2:2

The Bible is so special because it came from God. God speaks to us through the Bible and shows us how we can be close to Him by trusting in His Son, Jesus.

2 Corinthians 5:21; Ephesians 2:13; 1 Peter 2:24; 3:18

Thank you for letting me tell you about the Bible. I hope you will read your Bible so you can grow closer to God!

1 Peter 2:2

Also available in this series:

ISBN: 978-0-89221-614-7

ISBN: 978-0-89221-617-8

ISBN: 978-0-89221-616-1

Available at Christian bookstores nationwide

BiG Thoughts for Little Thinkers

BiG Thoughts for Little Thinkers
BiG Thoughts for Little Thinkers
BiG Thoughts for Little Thinkers
BiG Thoughts for Little Thinkers
BiG Thoughts for Little Thinkers
BiG Thoughts for Little Thinkers
BiG Thoughts for Little Thinkers